a collection of **sexy** quotes

a collection of **sexy** quotes

Michèle Brown

**Andrews McMeel
Publishing, LLC**

Kansas City

No part of this book may be used or reproduced in any manner whatsoever
without written permission except in the case of reprints in the context of reviews.
For information, write Andrews McMeel Publishing, LLC, an Andrews McMeel
Universal company, 4520 Main Street, Kansas City, Missouri 64111.

07 08 09 10 LEO 10 9 8 7 6 5 4 3 2

ISBN-13: 978-0-7407-6183-6
ISBN-10: 0-7407-6183-8

Library of Congress Control Number: 2006922714

www.andrewsmcmeel.com

ATTENTION: SCHOOLS AND BUSINESSES
Andrews McMeel books are available at quantity discounts with
bulk purchase for educational, business, or sales promotional use.
For information please write to:
Special Sales Department, Andrews McMeel Publishing, LLC,
4520 Main Street, Kansas City, Missouri 64111.

Introduction

Sex is as old as . . . well, if not the hills, at least as far back as the first time our earliest ancestors caught a twinkle in each other's eyes. Assuming the cigarette afterward still had a few hundred thousand millennia to go, we can only speculate what our primitive relatives thought about what they had been up to. When all was done, a lot remained to be said. But whatever passed between them, the way the human race has been riveted by sex ever since, anyone would think our lives depended on it.

This collection of words and wisdom captures quotes from vigorous enthusiasts between the sheets (and plenty of other places when the mood was right) and timid novices just coming to grips with one of life's great mysteries. Saucy, sage, and even occasionally sad, amorous icons like Brigitte Bardot (warmly remembered by former husband Roger Vadim) and diehard veterans like George Burns (who refused to give an inch to age when his passions were roused) explore the secrets, sentiments, and sensations that have inspired some of the most memorable and telling quips and quotes on sex.

The success (or otherwise) of the sex lives of those quoted remains (for the most part) a private matter—and a source of rich speculation. Spanning the centuries from ancient times to present day, they all have something fascinating to offer.

William Shakespeare gives voice to a universal frustration: "Is it not strange that desire should so many years outlive performance?" A century later, John Dryden was swept up by the positive power of sexual drive: "When beauty fires the blood, how love exalts the mind!"

Defining the difference between love and sex, Woody Allen laments: "Sex relieves tension and love causes it." Alexander Woolcott offers a definition of his own on the timeless art of sexual allure: "Nothing risqué, nothing gained."

Marlene Dietrich on the skills of seduction: "The longer they wait, the better they like it." Bette Davis would probably have agreed, judging by her acerbic remark on one Hollywood starlet for whom waiting was seldom an issue: "There goes the good time that's had by all."

Brought together, these words create an anthology in which celebrated writers rub shoulders with contemporary celebrities, and the sexually assured accompany those still trying to master the basics. In so doing they entertain the rest of us on every page.

Anyone who says he can see through women is missing a lot.

Groucho Marx

A mistress should be like a little country retreat near the town—not to dwell in constantly, but only for a night and away!
William Wycherley

Glances are the heavy artillery of the flirt: Everything can be conveyed in a look, yet that look can always be denied, for it cannot be quoted word for word.
Stendhal

There will be sex after death, we just won't be able to feel it.
Lily Tomlin

The sexual embrace can only be compared with music and with prayer.

Havelock Ellis

Amor vincit insomnia.

Unknown

There are some things that are better than bad sex: peanut butter and jelly. But in general, I can't think of anything better than good sex.

Billy Joel

If I told you you have a beautiful body, you wouldn't hold it against me, would you?

David Fisher

I was in San Francisco when the great earthquake struck, but we were kinda busy in the bedroom and we didn't notice what was going on outside.

John Barrymore

Whatever women do, they must do twice as well as men. Luckily, this is not difficult.

Charlotte Whitton

High heels were invented by a woman who had been kissed on the forehead.

Christopher Morley

Sex is as important as food and drink.

Britt Ekland

He who enjoys a good neighbor, said the Greeks, has a precious possession. Same goes for the neighbor's wife.

Nicholas Bentley

My girlfriend can count all the lovers she's had on one hand—if she's holding a calculator.

Tom Cotter

Eighty percent of American men cheat in America—the rest cheat in Europe.

Jackie Mason

On the topic of faked orgasms, if sex fraud were a crime, I'd be in jail for the rest of my life.

Merrill Markoe

I consider sex a misdemeanor—the more I miss, de meaner I get.

Mae West

Remember, if you smoke after sex you're doing it too fast.

Woody Allen

A girl can wait for the right man to come along, but in the meantime that still doesn't mean she can't have a wonderful time with all the wrong ones.

Cher

You can lead a horticulture but you cannot make her think.

Dorothy Parker

A dirty book
is rarely dusty.

Proverb

Nothing is better for the spirit
or the body than a love affair.
It elevates thoughts and
flattens stomachs.

Barbara Howar

When you have an affair with
a married man, you hear a lot
more about his wife than you
do about yourself.

Sandra Hochman

What is the difference between a bitch and a whore? A whore sleeps with everybody at a party, and a bitch sleeps with everybody at a party except you.

Unknown

Getting married for sex is like buying a 747 for the free peanuts.

Jeff Foxworthy

My breasts are beautiful, and I've got to tell you, they've gotten a lot of attention for what is relatively short screen time.

Jamie Lee Curtis

When authorities warn of the sinfulness of sex, there is an important lesson to be learned: Do not have sex with the authorities.

Matt Groening

No matter how happily a woman may be married, it always pleases her to discover that there is a nice man who wishes she were not.

Unknown

An erection at will is the moral equivalent of a valid credit card.

Alex Comfort

When a girl feels that she's perfectly groomed and dressed she can forget that part of her. That's charm. The more parts of yourself you can afford to forget the more charm you have.

F. Scott Fitzgerald

Long-legged girls are fascinating—built for walking through grass. Laurie Lee

Love means not ever having to say you're sorry.

Erich Segal

When people say, "You're breaking my heart," they do in fact usually mean that you're breaking their genitals.

Jeffrey Bernard

Love ain't
nothing
but sex
misspelled.

Harlan Ellison

Obscenity is
whatever
gives the
judge an
erection.

Graffito

It is an irony, appreciated only by
the French, that good manners
are the basis of very good sex. In
bed, the two most erotic words
in any language are "thank you"
and "please."

Hubert Downs

My girlfriend always laughs during sex—no matter what she's reading.
Steve Jobs

Some young Hollywood starlets remind me of my grandmother's old farmhouse—all painted up nice on the front side, a big swing on the backside, and nothing whatsoever in the attic.
Bette Davis

If God had meant for us to have group sex, he'd have given us more organs.
Malcolm Bradbury

Sex is a bad thing because it rumples the bedclothes.

Jackie Onassis

If you can't be a good example,
then you'll just have to be a horrible warning.
Catherine Aird

I would read *Playboy* magazine more often,
but my glasses keep steaming over.
George Burns

I wouldn't recommend sex, drugs, or insanity for everyone, but they've always worked for me.

Hunter S. Thompson

My dad told me, "Anything worth having is worth waiting for." I waited until I was fifteen.

Zsa Zsa Gabor

A wolf whistle is like a train whistle. You like to hear one even though you're not going anyplace.

Eloise McElhone

Nymphomaniac:
a woman as obsessed with sex as the average man.

Mignon McLaughlin

I'm just naturally respectful of pretty girls in tight-fitting sweaters.

Jack Parr

Next to the pleasure of taking a new mistress is that of being rid of an old one.

William Wycherley

A man can have two, maybe three, love affairs while he's married. But three is the absolute maximum. After that you're cheating.

Yves Montand

Love doesn't drop on you unexpectedly; you have to give off signals, sort of like an amateur radio operator.

Helen Gurley Brown

Sex is like snow: You never know how many inches you're going to get or how long it will last.

Unknown

I enjoy dating married men because they don't want anything kinky, like breakfast.

Joni Rodgers

The odds are usually 2:1 in favor of sex. You and she against her conscience.

Evan Esar

Love is like measles: We all have to go through it.

Jerome K. Jerome

Oysters are supposed to enhance your sexual performance, but they don't work for me. Maybe I put them on too soon.

Garry Shandling

Sex ought to be wholly a satisfying link between two affectionate people from which they emerge unanxious, rewarded, and ready for more.

Alex Comfort

Pornography is supposed to arouse sexual desires. If pornography is a crime, when will they arrest makers of perfume?
Richard Fleischer

Sex is like money.
Only too much is enough.
John Updike

It's great being blond—with such low expectations it's easy to impress.
Pamela Anderson

All the doors automatically open for a beautiful woman. I know it's very fashionable for good-looking ladies to say how hard it is to be beautiful, but that's not true.

Catherine Deneuve

There are only two superlative compliments you can receive from a woman. "I think you're a master chef" and "I think you're a great lay." The two basic drives in life.

Rod Steiger

Two minutes of gooey near satisfaction followed by two weeks of haunting guilt is so much more easily attained at Häagen-Dazs.

Florence Campbell

Personally, I like sex and I don't care what a man thinks of me as long as I get what I want from him— which is usually sex.

Valerie Perrine

Adultery is the most
conventional way
to rise above the
unconventional.

Vladimir Nabokov

My mother said it was simple to keep a man; you
must be a maid in the living room, a cook in the
kitchen, and a whore in the bedroom. I said I'd hire
the other two and take care of the bedroom bit.

Jerry Hall

I'm never through with a girl until I've had her three ways. John F. Kennedy

Garrison Keillor

Sex is good, but not as good as fresh sweet corn.

You sleep with a guy once and before you know it he wants to take you to dinner.

Myers Yori

Sex is the point of contact between man and nature, where morality and good intentions fall to primitive urges.

Camille Paglia

It was long accepted by the missionaries that morality was inversely proportional to the amount of clothing people wore.

Alex Carey

If you want to know the secret of my success with women, then don't smoke, don't take drugs, and don't be too particular.

George Best

I practice safe sex— I use an airbag.

Garry Shandling

Love is friendship plus sex.

Havelock Ellis

Love is time and space measured by the heart.

Marcel Proust

The best way to apply fragrance . . . is to spray it into the air . . . and walk into it.
Estée Lauder

The trouble with life is that there are so many beautiful women and so little time.
John Barrymore

Hearst come, Hearst served.
Marion Davies, mistress of William Randolph Hearst

**For me, love is very deep,
but sex only has to go a few inches.**
Stacy Nelkin

**I believe in censorship. After all,
I made a fortune out of it.**
Mae West

**Sex is not the answer. Sex is the
question. "Yes" is the answer.**
Swami X

Sex is more fun than cars, but cars refuel quicker than men.

Germaine Greer

Love is being stupid together.

Paul Valéry

Pornography is rather like trying to find out about a Beethoven symphony by having somebody tell you about it and perhaps hum a few bars.

Robertson Davies

The first day of spring was once the time for taking the young virgins into the fields, there in dalliance to set an example in fertility for nature to follow. Now we just set the clock an hour ahead and change the oil in the crankcase.

E. B. White

The most memorable one [of his many girlfriends] is always the current one; the rest just merge into a sea of blondes.

Rod Stewart

Make love to every woman you meet; if you get 5 percent on your outlay, it's a good investment.

Arnold Bennett

You have to accept that part of the sizzle of sex comes from the danger of sex. You can be overpowered.

Camille Paglia

White dresses make all suntanned girls seem beautiful.

Jimmy Cannon

Sweaty is sexy.

Farrah Fawcett

During sex my wife wants to talk to me. The other night she called me from a hotel.

Rodney Dangerfield

Today's unspeakable perversion is tomorrow's kink is next week's good clean fun.

Dab Savage

You must lay down
the treasures of
your body.

William Shakespeare

The hand on my knee was as warm as a bank account.

Kate Millett

**It's OK to laugh in the bedroom
so long as you don't point.**

Will Durst

I am always crazy for hot women. I am like a rabbit. I could do it anytime, anywhere.

Rod Stewart

For a long time I was ashamed of the way I lived. I didn't reform. I'm just not ashamed anymore.

Mae West

Nine cases out of ten, a woman had better show more affection than she feels.

Jane Austen

A girl's legs are her best friends, but the best of friends must part.

Redd Fox

No sex is better than bad sex.

Germaine Greer

In the past a sexy woman was one who lay on a sofa like an odalisque, smoking a cigarette. Now she is an athletic woman.

Hardy Amies

Never become involved with someone who can make you lose stature if your relationship becomes known. . . . Sleep up.

Aristotle Onassis

The difference between sex and love is that sex relieves tension and love causes it.

Woody Allen

The sexiest thing in the world is to be totally naked with your wedding band on.

Debra Winger

I need more sex, OK? Before I die I wanna taste everyone in the world.
Angelina Jolie

What matters is not the length of the wand but the magic in the stick.
Unknown

My idea of the ideal sex education site doesn't exist.
Susie Bright

When in doubt, wear red.
Bill Blass

I'd like to meet the man who invented sex and see what he's working on now.

Unknown

Love is like a game of poker. The girl, if she wants to win a hand that may affect her whole life, should be careful not to show her cards before the guy shows his.

Frank Sinatra

I never miss a chance to have sex or appear on television.

Gore Vidal

A chaste woman who teases is worse than a streetwalker. James G. Hunter

Abstinence is the mother of shameless lust.

Pat Califia

I think I could fall madly in bed with you.

Unknown

I'm saving the bass player for Omaha.

Janis Joplin

There are many things better than sex, but there's nothing quite like it.

W. C. Fields

Men aren't attracted to me by my mind. They're attracted by what I don't mind.

Gypsy Rose Lee

In my day hot pants were something we had, not wore.

Bette Davis

I haven't known any open marriages, although quite a few have been ajar.

Zsa Zsa Gabor

It's the good girls who keep the diaries; the bad girls never have the time.

Tallulah Bankhead

Sex appeal is 50 percent what you've got and 50 percent what you haven't got.

Sophia Loren

She's the kind of girl who climbed the ladder of success wrong by wrong.

Mae West

You know that look women get when they want sex? Me neither.
Drew Carey

I am the only man who can say he's been in Take That and at least two members of the Spice Girls.
Robbie Williams

It'll be a sad day for sexual liberation when the pornography addict has to settle for the real thing.
Brendan Francis

Lovemaking is a sublime art that needs practice if it's to be true and significant. But I suspect you're going to be an excellent student.

Charlie Chaplin

I bought my wife a sex manual but half the pages were missing. We went straight from foreplay to post-natal depression.

Bob Monkhouse

I once had a rose named after me and I was very flattered. But I was not pleased to read the description in the catalog: no good in bed, but fine up against a wall.

Eleanor Roosevelt

There is no unhappier creature on earth than a fetishist who yearns for a woman's shoe and has to embrace the whole woman.

Karl Kraus

The big difference between sex for money and sex for free is that sex for money usually costs a lot less.

Brendan Francis

A date, at this juncture in history, is any prearranged meeting with the opposite sex toward whom you have indecent intentions.... One does not need to sleep with, or even touch, someone who has paid for your meal. All those obligations are hereby rendered null and void, and any man who doesn't think so needs a quick jab in the kidneys.

Cynthia Heimel

For a woman to be loved, she usually ought to be naked. Pierre Cardin

Unknown

Pornography is in the groin of the beholder.

Sex is perhaps like culture—a luxury that only becomes an art after generations of leisurely acceptance.

Alice B. Toklas

A bachelor lives like a king
and dies like a beggar.

L. S. Lowry

Men who aren't pet lovers
aren't any good in bed.

Jilly Cooper

Be wary of puppy love; it can
lead to a dog's life.

Gladiola Montana

Love is the same as like except you feel sexier.

Judith Viorst

A little coitus never hoitus.

Graffito

The girl had as many curves as a scenic railway.

P. G. Wodehouse

As for not sleeping with the boss, why discriminate against him?

Helen Gurley Brown

One night with her [Brigitte Bardot] was worth a lifetime.

Roger Vadim

He was the kind of guy who could kiss you behind your ear and make you feel like you'd just had kinky sex.

Julia Alvarez

It is difficult to see why lace should be so expensive; it's mostly holes.

Mary Wilson Little

He said, "I can't remember when we last had sex," and I said, "Well I can and that's why we ain't doing it."

Roseanne Barr

Orgy: a party where everybody comes.

Unknown

I haven't met him but I send him naked pictures.

Sheena Easton

Hardly anyone marries when they're in love—they're in heat.

William Lederer

To the average male there is seemingly nothing so attractive or so challenging as a reasonably good-looking young mother who is married and alone.

Shirley MacLaine

Sex is bad for one—but it's very good for two.

Graffito

There's nothing wrong with a woman welcoming all men's advances, darling, as long as they are in cash.

Zsa Zsa Gabor

"Where should one use perfume?" a young woman asked. "Wherever one wants to be kissed," I said.

Coco Chanel

His voice was as intimate as the rustle of sheets.

Dorothy Parker

Losing my virginity was a career move.

Madonna

There is only one real tragedy in a woman's life. The fact that her past is always her lover, and her future is always her husband.

Oscar Wilde

A beautiful woman seductively dressed will never catch cold no matter how low cut her gown.

Friedrich Nietzsche

Two is company.
Three is fifty bucks.

Joan Rivers

Sex is like art. Most of it is pretty bad, and the good stuff is out of your price range.

Scott Roeben

Some men are all right in their place— if they only knew the right places.

Mae West

Courtship is to marriage
as a very witty prologue
is to a dull play.

William Congreve

One does not take the wife of
the man that feeds you, even
if it is only for one afternoon.

Taki Theodoracopulos

The real fountain of
youth is to have a
dirty mind.

Jerry Hall

Glamour is when a man knows a woman is a woman.

Gina Lollobrigida

Macho does not prove mucho.

Zsa Zsa Gabor

Sex without love is as hollow and ridiculous as love without sex.

Hunter S. Thompson

Plunging necklines attract more attention and cost less money.

Shelley Winters

Why are women wearing perfumes that smell like flowers? Men don't like flowers. I've been wearing a great new scent guaranteed to attract men. It's called New Car Interior.

Rita Rudner

A kiss can be a comma, a question mark, or an exclamation point. That's basic spelling that every woman ought to know.
Minstinguett

Just because a man has something that sticks out doesn't mean he's got to put it anywhere and everywhere.
Goldie Hawn

The only difference between friends and lovers is about four minutes.
Scott Roeben

Most beautiful but dumb girls think they are smart and get away with it, because other people, on the whole, aren't much smarter.

Louise Brooks

It would be less demanding, enslaving, perplexing, and strenuous for a healthy male to screw a thousand women in his lifetime than to try to please one, and the potential for failure would be less.

Irma Kurtz

Copulation was, I'm sure, Marilyn's [Monroe] uncomplicated way of saying thank you.

Nunnaly Johnson

Whoever named it necking was a poor judge of anatomy.

Groucho Marx

I'm a terrible lover—I've actually given a woman an anticlimax.

Scott Roeben

Acting is like sex. You should do it, not talk about it.

Joanne Woodward

I find men terribly exciting and any girl who says she doesn't is an old maid, a streetwalker, or a saint.

Lana Turner

He was one of those men who come in the door and make any woman with them look guilty.

F. Scott Fitzgerald

God made men stronger but not necessarily more intelligent. He gave women intuition and femininity. And, used properly, that combination easily jumbles the brain of any man I've ever met.

Farrah Fawcett

Marriage is popular because it combines the maximum of temptation with the maximum of opportunity.

George Bernard Shaw

It is easier to keep half a dozen lovers guessing than to keep one lover after he has stopped guessing.

Helen Rowland

They are doing things on the screen these days that the French don't even put on postcards.

Bob Hope

Men like long nails; in old movies
couples were always scratching
each other's backs.
Britt Ekland

I prefer the old miniskirt to the slit
skirt. . . . You don't have to be so alert.
Bob Thaves

I really am a cat transferred into a
woman. . . . I purr. I scratch.
And sometimes I bite.
Brigitte Bardot

Word to the wise for men: Although meant as a compliment, "You make love like a professional" isn't always received as such.

Derek Cockram

I love those slow-talking southern girls. I was out with a southern girl last night. Took her so long to tell me she wasn't that kind of girl, she was.

Woody Woodbury

The only unnatural sex act is that which you cannot perform.

Dr. Alfred Kinsey

After making love I said to my girl, "Was it good for you, too?" And she said, "I don't think this was good for anybody."

Garry Shandling

Is that a gun in your pocket or are you just glad to see me?

Mae West

Sex is. There is nothing more to be done about it. Sex builds no roads, writes no novels, and sex certainly gives no meaning to anything in life but itself.

Gore Vidal

If women didn't exist, all the money in the world would have no meaning.
Aristotle Onassis

Zsa Zsa Gabor

Men love with their eyes; women love with their ears.

The psychiatrist asked me if I thought sex was dirty and I said, "It is if you're doing it right."

Woody Allen

If you have a good relationship, that's all the more reason to want to have another good one. Which is what the trouble is.

John Irving

I told her the thing I loved most about her was her mind … because that's what told her to get into bed with me naked.

Steven Wright

Everybody's attracted to sex. So I'm learning to use it a lot better than I used to because if we ain't using it, we're wasting it.

Kim Basinger

You never know a man until you know how he loves.

Sigmund Freud

She who is silent consents.

French proverb

Don't stint on the foreplay. Be inventive.

Dr. Ruth Westheimer

One man's remorse is another man's reminiscence.
Gerald Horton Bath

Sexual intercourse is kicking death in the ass while singing.
Charles Bukowski

In adolescence, pornography is a
substitute for sex, whereas in
adulthood, sex is a substitute
for pornography.
Edmund White

Love is its own aphrodisiac and is the
main ingredient for lasting sex.
Mort Katz

I'm finished with men,
but I have a very full memory.
Ursula Andress

The longer they wait, the better they like it.

Marlene Dietrich

Sex without love is merely healthy exercise.

Robert A. Heinlein

Sex is more exciting on the screen and between the pages than between the sheets.

Andy Warhol

It's hard to take showers with only one of the five guys you are dating.

Cher

Perhaps at fourteen every boy should be in love with some ideal woman to put on a pedestal and worship. As he grows up, of course, he will put her on a pedestal the better to view her legs.

Barry Norman

You'd be surprised how much better a man gets when you know he's worth $150 million.

Joan Rivers

When choosing between two evils, I always like to take the one I've never tried before.

Mae West

Most women feel like a virgin each time they make love to someone who matters.

Linda Taylor

A curved line is the loveliest distance between two points.

Mae West

I don't breed well in captivity.

Gloria Steinem

You know more about a man in one night in bed than you do in months of conversation. In the sack, they can't cheat.

Edith Piaf

You know what comes between me and my Calvins? Nothing.

Brooke Shields

I love men, I love sex, and I don't care who knows it.

Margot Kidder

A fool and her money are soon courted.

Helen Rowland

Sex drive: a physical craving that begins in adolescence and ends in marriage.

Robert Byrne

A woman begins by resisting a man's advances and ends by blocking his retreat.

Oscar Wilde

In love as in sport, the amateur status must be strictly maintained.

Robert Graves

I do a lot of research, especially in the apartments of tall blondes.

Raymond Chandler

All men are different, but husbands are all alike.

William Howard Taft

Bed is the poor man's opera.

Italian proverb

I guess a film in which I didn't end up in bed, in the sea, or in a hot tub would have the same appeal as a Clint Eastwood movie in which nobody got shot.

Bo Derek

There are things that happen in the dark between two people that make everything that happens in the light seem all right.

Erica Jong

It may be discovered someday that an orgasm actually lasts for hours and only seems like a few seconds.

Dolly Parton

Women's fashion is a subtle form of bondage. It's men's way of binding them. We put them in these tight, high-heeled shoes, we make them wear these tight clothes, and we say they look sexy. But they're actually tied up.

David Duchovny

I say I don't sleep with married men,
but what I mean is that I don't sleep
with happily married men.

Britt Ekland

Husbands are like fires—
they go out when unattended.

Zsa Zsa Gabor

Sex can be fun after eighty,
after ninety, and after lunch.

George Burns

I knew I would like her when I saw how her backside moved under her red satin skirt.

James Hadley Chase

My ultimate fantasy is to entice a man to my bedroom, put a gun to his head, and say, "Make babies or die."

Ruby Wax

I don't remember the first kiss. I remember the first good kiss.

Angie Dickinson

Sex stops when you pull up your pants; love never lets go. Kingsley Amis

Take off the shell with your clothes.

Alex Comfort

No matter what a woman looks like, if she's confident, she's sexy.

Paris Hilton

Lord give me chastity— but not yet.

St. Augustine

One of the paramount reasons for staying attractive is so you can have somebody to go to bed with.

Helen Gurley Brown

Cannes is where you lie on the beach and stare at the stars— or vice versa.

Rex Reed

Sexiness in a woman is certainly a redeeming social value.

Peter Bogdanovich

The movie business divides women into ice queens and sluts, and there have been times I wanted to be a slut more than anything.

Sigourney Weaver

If you have a vagina and an attitude in this town, then that's a lethal combination.

Sharon Stone

There are two good reasons why men will go to see her [Jane Russell].

Howard Hughes

Love is blind; that is why it always proceeds by the sense of touch.

French proverb

I'll tell you what I don't like about Christmas office parties—looking for a new job afterward.
Phyllis Diller

How he looks in a bathing suit should not be discounted. The fact is, I stare at men quite a lot.
Jane Fonda

No matter how much cats fight, there always seem to be plenty of kittens.
Abraham Lincoln

Love is the answer, but while you are waiting for the answer, sex raises some pretty good questions.

Woody Allen

If you have been married more than ten years, being good in bed means you don't steal the covers.

Brenda Davidson

The trouble with some women is that they get all excited about nothing, and then they marry him.

Cher

Girls have an unfair advantage over men. If they can't get what they want being smart, they can get it by being dumb.

Yul Brynner

It is not sex that gives the pleasure, but the lover.

Marge Piercy

I think there's something incredibly sexy about a woman wearing her boyfriend's T-shirt and underwear.

Calvin Klein

I need sex for a clear complexion, but I'd rather do it for love. Joan Crawford

Evan Esar

In the art of love it is more important to know when than how.

We waste time looking for the perfect lover, instead of creating the perfect love.

Tom Robbins

Our biological drives are
several million years older
than our intelligence.

Arthur E. Morgan

To me a woman's body is a
temple. I try to attend services
as often as I can.

Will Shriner

I carried my Oscar to bed with
me. My first and only three-
way happened that night.

Halle Berry

When a woman is speaking to you,
listen to what she says with her eyes.

Victor Hugo

You'd be surprised how much it costs to look cheap.

Dolly Parton

She was the original good time that was had by all.

Bette Davis

Man has his will—but woman has her way.

Oliver Wendell Holmes

We made civilization in order to impress our girlfriends.

Orson Welles

Marriage, if it is to survive,
must be treated as the beginning,
not as the happy ending.
Federico Fellini

Love at first sight may be possible,
but I feel a lot stronger about
lust at first sight.
Xaviera Hollander

Men want women they can turn on
and off like a light switch.
Ian Fleming

I like to wake up feeling a new man.

Jean Harlow

The ends justify the jeans.

Graffito

You don't have to have a language in common with someone for a sexual rapport. But it helps if the language you don't understand is Italian.

Madonna

To my gorgeous lover, Harry. I'll trade all my It for your that.

Clara Bow, inscribed by the "It" girl on a photograph for her fiancé Harry Richman

When a man talks dirty to a woman, it's sexual harassment. When a woman talks dirty to a man, it's $3.95 a minute.

Steven Wright

Marriage is the deep, deep peace of the double bed after the hurly-burly of the chaise longue.

Mrs. Patrick Campbell

When things don't work well in the bedroom, they don't work well in the living room, either.

Dr. William H. Masters

All women do have a different sense of sexuality, or sense of fun, or sense of what's sexy or cool or tough.

Angelina Jolie

I never made any money until I took my pants off.

Sally Rand

Hair is another name for sex.

Vidal Sassoon

Among men, sex sometimes results in intimacy; among women, intimacy sometimes results in sex.

Barbara Cartland

When a man and woman of unorthodox tastes make love, the man could be said to be introducing his foible into her quirk.

Kenneth Tynan

If the world were a logical place, men would ride sidesaddle.

Rita Mae Brown

Absinthe makes the parts grow stronger.

Jack Hibberd

Women prefer men who have something tender about them—especially the legal kind.

Kay Ingram

I was the good Bond girl, but I wanted to have the dresses and the high heels. I wanted the funky, sexy name.

Izabella Scorupco

The gravity is very light today. I have an erection as a result of that. All males have erections on days like this.

Kurt Vonnegut

Sex concentrates on what is on the outside of the individual. It's funny because I think it's better on the inside.

Alex Walsh

Sailing is like screwing: You can never get enough.

Brigitte Bardot

Sex is the gateway to life.

Frank Harris

Older women are best because they think they might be doing it for the last time.

Ian Fleming

Beauty without grace is the hook without the bait.

Ralph Waldo Emerson

Every man wants a woman to appeal to his better side, his nobler instincts, and his higher nature—and another woman to help him forget them.

Helen Rowland

When a guy goes to a hooker,
he's not paying her for sex,
he's paying her to leave.
Unknown

Of all the delights of this world,
man cares most for sexual intercourse.
Yet he has left it out of his heaven.
Mark Twain

Brevity is the soul of lingerie.
Dorothy Parker

All a writer has to do to get a woman is to say he's a writer. It's an aphrodisiac.

Saul Bellow

It was never dirty to me. After all, God gave us the equipment and the opportunity. There's that old saying, "If God had meant us to fly, he'd have given us wings." Well, look what he did give us.

Dolly Parton

It is impossible to become bored in the presence of a mistress.

Stendhal

One does not fall in or out of love. One grows in love. Leo Buscaglia

I like men to behave like men— strong and childish.

Françoise Sagan

She's been on more laps than a napkin.

Walter Winchell

Sex is hardly ever just about sex.

Shirley MacLaine

There's something incredibly sexy about sand and sweat and dunes photographed like women's backs.

Kristin Scott Thomas

To me love is being able to go to bed with someone and feel better about them when you wake up the next morning.

Sylvester Stallone

Love is a matter of chemistry, but sex is a matter of physics.

Unknown

"Sex" is as important as eating or drinking, and we ought to allow the one appetite to be satisfied with as little restraint or false modesty as the other.

Marquis de Sade

My problem is that girls are always running through my mind. Considering my thoughts, they wouldn't dare walk.

Andy Gibb

Before I married my husband, I'd never fallen in love, though I'd stepped in it a few times.

Rita Rudner

Las Vegas showgirls: They're naked from the waist up, wearing a G-string, and say, "I'm a very private person."

Joan Rivers

I like exposing myself. There's not
an awful lot that embarrasses me.
I'm the kind of actress who absolutely
believes in exposing herself.
Kate Winslet

Husbands are chiefly good lovers
when they are betraying their wives.
Marilyn Monroe

My trouble is reconciling my
gross habits with my net income.
Errol Flynn

If I've still got my pants on in the second scene, I think they've sent me the wrong script.

Mel Gibson

It's not true that I had nothing on. I had the radio on.

Marilyn Monroe

It is better to be unfaithful than to be faithful without wanting to be.

Brigitte Bardot

Love is not the dying moan of a distant violin, it's the triumphant twang of a bedspring.

S. J. Perelman

No woman is so naked as one you can see to be naked underneath her clothes.

Michael Frayn

In sex as in banking there is a penalty for early withdrawal.

Cynthia Nelms

There's nothing worse than the girl who is considered charmless, except the man who is considered harmless.

Evan Esar

If you're good in bed at home, why not do it in public? Jim Petersen

Rodney Dangerfield

At certain times I like sex—like after a cigarette.

They made love as if they were an endangered species.

Peter de Vries

The longest absence is less
perilous to love than
the terrible trials of
incessant proximity.

Ouida

An erection is like the
Theory of Relativity: The
more you think about it,
the harder it gets.

Graffito

What men call gallantry,
and gods adultery, is much
more common where the
climate's sultry.

Lord Byron

Good girls go to heaven; bad girls go everywhere.

Helen Gurley Brown

If a thing loves, it is infinite.

William Blake

Imagination is more important than knowledge.

Albert Einstein

Sex is like money: very nice to have but vulgar to talk about.

Tonia Berg

Never in the history of sex has so much been offered to so many by so few.

Quentin Crisp

One more drink and I'd be under the host.
Dorothy Parker

My biggest sex fantasy is we're making
love and I realize I'm out of debt.
Beth Lapides

Warren [Beatty] could handle women
as smoothly as operating an elevator.
He knew exactly where to locate
the top button. One flick and
we were on our way.
Britt Ekland

It's true that the French have a certain obsession with sex, but it's a particularly adult obsession. France is the thriftiest of all nations; to a Frenchman sex provides the most economical way to have fun.

Anita Loos

An orgasm a day keeps the doctor away.

Mae West

It's an extra dividend when you like the girl you're in love with.

Clark Gable

Is it a man walking on the beach, winking at the girls and looking for going to bed? Is it someone who wears a lot of gold chains and rings and sits at the bar? Because this is not me! I am very, very Latin, but not so much lover.

Antonio Banderas

How do girls get minks? The same way minks get minks.

Graffito

From the moment I was six I felt sexy. And let me tell you it was hell, sheer hell, waiting to do something about it.

Bette Davis

A dress makes no sense unless it inspires men to want to take it off you.

Françoise Sagan

Nobody will ever win the battle of the sexes; there's too much fraternizing with the enemy.

Henry Kissinger

Happiness is watching TV at your girlfriend's house during a power failure.

Bob Hope

She gave me a smile I could feel in my hip pocket.

Raymond Chandler

He sleeps fastest who sleeps alone.

Richard Avedon

I like my sex the way I play basketball: one on one with as little dribbling as possible.

Leslie Nielsen

The first breath of adultery is the freest; after it, constraints aping marriage develop.

John Updike

Personally, I like a woman to be a whore in bed.

Bruce Dern

A country without bordellos is like a house without bathrooms.

Marlene Dietrich

Nothing risqué, nothing gained.

Alexander Woolcott

It's been so long since I made love, I can't even remember who gets tied up.

Joan Rivers

I am not easily aroused. For me it takes quite a long time until the first kiss.

Jennifer Lopez

The reason people sweat is so they won't catch fire when making love.

Don Rose

Outside every thin girl there is a fat man trying to get in.

Katherine Whitehorn

I used to be Snow White, but I drifted.

Mae West

Once they call you a Latin lover, you're in real trouble. Women expect an Oscar performance in bed.

Marcello Mastroianni

The rapture of seeing braless women jogging can inspire me to run another five miles or so. The jogging bra is the worst invention since nuclear weapons.

Richard Smith

A great social success is a pretty girl who plays her cards as carefully as if she were plain.

F. Scott Fitzgerald

Sometimes it's Britney Spears and sometimes it's Carrie Fisher. I can't tell if I've got a Lolita complex or an Oedipus complex.

Ben Affleck

Sex will outlive us all.
Samuel Goldwyn

A woman should be obscene,
and not heard.
Groucho Marx

The mirror tells only the facts,
never the poetry.
May Sarton

Chocolate for me is just like an orgasm.

Britney Spears

Sex without love is an empty experience, but, as empty experiences go, it's one of the best.

Woody Allen

She [Maureen O'Hara] looked as if butter wouldn't melt in her mouth—or anywhere else.

Elsa Lanchester

What man desires is a virgin who is a whore.

Karl Kraus

I love football, it's the second best thing in the world. **Joe Namath**

If it is not erotic, it is not interesting.

Fernando Arrabal

I feel like a million tonight. But one at a time.

Mae West

If you aren't going all the way, why go at all?

Joe Namath

A little incompatibility is the spice of life, particularly if he has income and she is pattable.

Ogden Nash

The best things in life are free.... Try explaining that to an angry prostitute.

Daniel Bokor

There are two things I like stiff—and one of them's Jell-O.

Dame Nellie Melba

I would like to suggest that, at least on the face of it, a stroke-by-stroke story of copulation is exactly as absurd as a chew-by-chew account of the consumption of a chicken wing.

William Gass

Sex, treated properly, can be one of the most gorgeous things in the world.

Elizabeth Taylor

Pleasure is the object, the duty, the goal of all rational creatures.

Voltaire

Sex is like money, golf, and beer—even when it's bad, it's good.

Jimmy Williams

I may not be Fred Flintstone,
but I can make your bed rock.
Unknown

Gentlemen always seem
to remember blondes.
Anita Loos

Of course, chicks keep popping up.
When you're in a hotel, a pretty young
lady makes life bearable.
Roger Daltrey

Anything that can't be done in bed isn't worth doing at all.

Groucho Marx

What do atheists scream when they come?

Bill Hicks

I generally avoid temptation unless I can't resist it.

Mae West

One is very crazy when in love.

Sigmund Freud

Erogenous zones are either everywhere or nowhere.

Joseph Heller

It's not the men in my life, it's the life in my men.

Mae West

For women the best aphrodisiacs are words. The G-spot is in the ears. He who looks for it below there is wasting his time.

Isabel Allende

It's the fallen women who are usually picked up. Woody Allen

Virginia Woolf

The older one grows the more one likes indecency.

Women: You can't live with them, you can't live without them. That's probably why you can rent one for the evening.

Jim Stark

What is a promiscuous person? It's usually someone who is getting more sex than you are.

Victor Lownes

Young men still desire women as much as ever, even though they don't want to marry them as much.

Clare Boothe Luce

Isn't it interesting how the sounds are the same for an awful nightmare and great sex?

Rue McClanahan

Sleeping with Kurt Cobain is worth a half million dollars.

Courtney Love

A hard man is good to find.

Mae West

Sex at age ninety is like trying to shoot pool with a rope.

George Burns

Sex hasn't been the same since women started to enjoy it.

Lewis Grizzard

There are two reasons why I'm in show business, and I'm standing on both of them.

Betty Grable

What turns me on? Tuesday Weld
in a dirty slip drinking beer.
Alice Cooper

The language of sex is yet to be
invented. The language of the senses
is yet to be explored.
Anaïs Nin

When she raises her eyelids it's as if
she were taking off all her clothes.
Colette

Thanks, I enjoyed every inch of it.

Mae West

The backseat produced the sexual revolution.

Jerry Rubin

Kissing, petting, and even intercourse are all right as long as they are sincere. I have never given a kiss in my life that wasn't sincere. As for intercourse, I'd say three times a night was about right.

Margaret Sanger

Sex on television can't hurt you unless you fall off.

Bumper sticker

I came from a generation where you knew nothing. You learned by doing. . . . I thought you took turns moving. Whoever had the good position moved.

Joan Rivers

Sex is one of the nine reasons for reincarnation. The other eight are unimportant.

Henry Miller

Women might be able to fake orgasms, but men can fake a whole relationship.

Sharon Stone

Women are like ovens. We need five to fifteen minutes to heat up.

Sandra Bullock

I don't try to be a sex bomb. I am one.

Kylie Minogue

An improper mind is a perpetual feast.

Logan Persall Smith

Chivalry: going about releasing beautiful maidens from other men's castles and taking them to your own castle.

Henry W. Nevinson

Using Viagra is like putting a new flagpole on a condemned building.

Harvey Korman

Save a boyfriend for a rainy day and another in case it doesn't.

Mae West

Kinky is using a feather.
Perverted is using the whole chicken.

Unknown

Her kisses left something to be desired—the rest of her.

Unknown

Continental people have a sex life; the English have hot water bottles.

George Mikes

At my age, I want two girls at once. I fall asleep, they have each other to talk to.

Rodney Dangerfield

Like the measles, love is most dangerous when it comes late in life.

Lord Byron

There are no chaste minds. Minds copulate wherever they meet.

Eric Hoffer

Once a philosopher, twice a pervert.

Voltaire

Be careful what you show—and what you don't show.

Marlene Dietrich

Underwear is such an emotional thing.

Elle MacPherson

A woman … should be like a good suspense movie: The more left to the imagination the more excitement there is. This should be her aim—to create suspense.

Alfred Hitchcock

I kissed my first woman and smoked
my first cigarette on the same day.
I haven't had time for tobacco since.
Arturo Toscanini

Testosterone does not
have to be toxic.
Anna Quindlen

If sex is such a natural phenomenon,
how come there are so many
books on how to?
Bette Midler

I think the reason guys like women in leather outfits so much is because they have that new-car smell.

George Fara

She said he proposed something on their wedding night that even her own brother wouldn't have suggested.

James Thurber

I knew at once that Rock Hudson was gay when he did not fall in love with me.

Gina Lollobrigida

Sex is conversation carried out by other means. **Peter Ustinov**

I've always looked better lying down.

Jerry Hall

Is it not strange that desire should so many years outlive performance?

William Shakespeare

Love letters are the campaign promises of the heart.

Robert Friedman

My classmates would copulate with anything that moved, but I never saw any reason to limit myself.

Emo Philips

What a man enjoys about a woman's clothes are his fantasies of how she would look without them.

Evelyn Waugh

The fifties was the most sexually frustrated decade ever: ten years of foreplay.

Lily Tomlin

Money, it turned out, was exactly like sex: You thought of nothing else if you didn't have it and thought of other things if you did.

James Baldwin

It was a blonde. A blonde to make a bishop kick a hole in a stained-glass window.

Raymond Chandler

Why is food better than men? Because you don't have to wait an hour for seconds.

Unknown

Few men know how to kiss well; fortunately, I've always had time to teach them.

Mae West

I once made love for an hour and fifteen minutes. But it was the night the clocks were set ahead.

Garry Shandling

A bikini is like a barbed wire fence. It protects the property without obstructing the view.

Joey Adams

In love, as in gluttony, pleasure is a matter of the utmost precision.

Italo Calvino

Seamed stockings aren't subtle but they certainly do the job. You shouldn't wear them with someone you're not prepared to sleep with, since their presence is tantamount to saying, "Hi there, big fellow, please rip my clothes off at your earliest opportunity." If you really want your escort paralytic with lust, stop frequently to adjust the seams.

Cynthia Heimel

See, the problem is that God gives men a brain and a penis, and only enough blood to run one at a time.

Robin Williams

They say if you have positive thoughts about something, it will happen. Well, I've been thinking positively about my neighbor's nineteen-year-old daughter, but so far, no luck. I think maybe my wife's negative thoughts are interfering.

Maurizio Mariotti

It's so hard for an old rake to turn over a new leaf.

John Barrymore

Sex is just another real good drug… and it can make a junkie out of you. It can grab you by the throat.

Elizabeth Ashley

In my sex fantasy, nobody ever loves me for my mind. **Nora Ephron**

Mae West

Too much of a good thing is wonderful.

The angle of the dangle is proportional to the heat of the meat provided that the urge to surge remains constant.

Unknown

There is no greater fan of the opposite sex, and I have the bills to prove it.

Alan Jay Lerner

Men make love more intensely at twenty but make love better at thirty.

Catherine II of Russia

In sexual intercourse it's quality not quantity that counts.

Dr. David Reuben

I know so much about men because I went to night school.

Mae West

Sex is part of nature. I go along with nature.

Marilyn Monroe

I like the whiskey old and the women young.

Errol Flynn

I consider a day in which I make love only once virtually wasted.
Porfirio Rubirosa

Dancing is a perpendicular expression of a horizontal desire.
George Bernard Shaw

Most plain girls are virtuous because
of the scarcity of opportunity
to be otherwise.
Maya Angelou

There are no good girls gone wrong,
just bad girls found out.
Mae West

The only reason I would take up
jogging is so that I could hear
heavy breathing again.
Erma Bombeck

When you sleep with someone you take off a lot more than your clothes.

Anna Quindlen

Sex is emotion in motion.

Mae West

Kathy Sue Loudermilk was a lovely child and a legend before her sixteenth birthday. She was twenty-one, however, before she knew an automobile had a front seat.

Lewis Grizzard

Pursuit and seduction are the essence of sexuality. It's part of the sizzle.

Camille Paglia

Sex gives us a glimpse or a concentration of the mind that would make us godlike if we could command it in other spheres.

Colin Wilson

If goodness is its own reward, shouldn't we get a little something for being naughty?

Lauren Bacall

Ecology is like sex: Every new generation likes to think they were the first to discover it.

Michael Allaby

A lover has all the good points and all the bad points that are lacking in a husband.

Honoré de Balzac

A lady is one who never shows her underwear unintentionally.

Lillian Day

I'm interested in pushing people's buttons.

Madonna

Retrospectively, I would agree with Luis Buñuel that sex without sin is like an egg without salt.

Carlos Fuentes

Anybody who believes that the way to a man's heart is through his stomach flunked geography.

Robert Byrne

I think making love is the best form of exercise.

Cary Grant

The trouble with nude dancing is that not everything stops when the music stops.
Robert Helpman

The only time human beings are sane is the ten minutes after intercourse.
Eric Berne

Sex is a natural function. You can't make it happen, but you can teach people to let it happen.

Dr. William H. Masters

This country is into tits and ass.

Neil Simon

The mistakes you regret the most in your life are the ones you didn't commit when you had the chance.

Helen Rowland

Lead me not into temptation. I can find the way myself.

Rita Mae Brown

There's nothing wrong with a person's sex life that the right psychoanalyst can't exaggerate.

Gerald Horton Bath

Being a sex symbol has to do with an attitude, not looks. Most men think it's looks, most women know otherwise.

Kathleen Turner

Conservatives say teaching sex education in the public schools will promote promiscuity. With our education system? If we promote promiscuity the same way we promote math or science, they've got nothing to worry about.

Beverly Michins

I like naked ladies—one at a time, in private.

Bernard Levin

Anyone who calls it "sexual intercourse" can't possibly be interested in doing it. You might as well announce you're ready for lunch by proclaiming, "I'd like to do some masticating and enzyme secreting."

Allan Sherman

Young men want to be faithful,
and are not; old men want
to be faithless, and cannot.

Oscar Wilde

Men are those creatures
with two legs and eight hands.

Jane Mansfield

Nothing will make a model
husband faster than infidelity.

Peter de Vries

One should always be in love. That is the reason one should never marry.

Oscar Wilde

Disco provides a rhythmic accompaniment for the activities of people who wish to gain access to each other for potential future reproduction.

Frank Zappa

Were kisses all the joys in bed, one woman would another wed.

William Shakespeare

I have always been discriminating in my choice of lovers, but once in bed I am like a slave. **Britt Ekland**

When beauty fires the blood, how love exalts the mind!

John Dryden

A genuine kiss generates so much heat it destroys germs.

Dr. S. L. Katzoff

Virtue is not photogenic.

Kirk Douglas

It takes a woman twenty years to make a man of her son and another woman twenty minutes to make a fool of him.

Helen Rowland

There's nothing inherently dirty about sex, but if you try real hard and use your imagination you can overcome that.

Lewis Grizzard

If truth is beauty, how come no one has their hair done in the library?

Lily Tomlin

To lovers, touch is metamorphosis. All the parts of their bodies seem to change, and seem to become something different and better.

John Cheever

The first thrill of adultery is entering the house. Everything there has been paid for by the other man.

John Updike

The sexual drive is nothing but the motor memory of previously experienced pleasure.

Wilhelm Reich

Some people have flat feet. Some people have dandruff. I have this appalling imagination.

Tom Ewell

The penis is mightier than the sword.
Mark Twain

A bachelor gets tangled up with
a lot of women in order to avoid
getting tied to one.
Helen Rowland

Women were born with a sense
of humor so they could love men
and not laugh at them.
Graffito

A man has missed something if he has never woken up in an anonymous bed beside a face he'll never see again, and if he has never left a brothel at dawn feeling like jumping off a bridge into the river out of sheer physical disgust with life.

Gustave Flaubert

They look like real ladies who can let go and become tigers in the bedroom. Blondes give the impression that whatever they do, they do with gusto.

Alfred Hitchcock

A woman can look both moral and exciting... if she also looks as if it was quite a struggle.

Edna Ferber

I loved Kirk [the Mormon missionary she kidnapped, chained to a bed, and forced to have sex with her] so much I would have skied down Mount Everest in the nude with a carnation up my nose.

Joyce McKinney

I dress for women and
undress for men.

Angie Dickinson

Your words are my food, your breath my wine.
You are everything to me.

Sarah Bernhardt

It is not enough to conquer; one must know
how to seduce. **Voltaire**

Mae West

To err is human, but it feels divine.

Women with pasts interest men because they hope history will repeat itself.

Mae West

The difference between pornography and erotica is lighting.

Gloria Leonard

Power is a great aphrodisiac and I'm a very powerful person.

Madonna

I thank God I was raised Catholic, so sex will always be dirty.

John Waters

Beauty isn't everything! But then what is?

Lanford Wilson

Marriage is a mistake every man should make.

George Jersel

I wish I had as much in bed as I get in the newspapers.

Linda Ronstadt

Love is so much better when you are not married.

Maria Callas

You must not force sex to do the work of love or love to do the work of sex.

Mary McCarthy

If the young only knew;
if the old only could.
French proverb

A little still she strove, and much
repented, And whispering "I will
ne'er consent"—consented.
Lord Byron, *Don Juan*

If you are ever in doubt as to whether or
not you should kiss a pretty girl, always
give her the benefit of the doubt.
Thomas Carlyle

There are three things a man can do with women: love them, suffer for them, or turn them into literature.

Stephen Stills

I don't need a psychiatrist, I need a man.

Marilyn Monroe

Even when I was a kid, the *Bolero* was always something that you bought in a brown paper bag, because people knew what you were going to use it for.

Henry Mancini

I haven't had that many women—only as many as I could lay my hands on.

Dudley Moore

Knowing what I do now about women, if I could just travel back in time to when I was sixteen years old, I bet I would have gotten laid by now.

Ed Smith

The supreme happiness in life is the conviction of being loved not *for* yourself, but in *spite* of yourself.

Victor Hugo

Men read maps better because only a male mind could conceive of an inch equaling a hundred miles.

Roseanne Barr

You know what charm is: a way of getting the answer "yes" without having asked any clear question.

Albert Camus

Why don't you come up sometime, and see me?

Mae West

Ten days of abstinence awakens passion.

Ricardo Montalban

When a man goes on a date, he wonders if he is going to get lucky. A woman already knows.

Frederike Ryder

If I were asked for a one-line answer to the question "What makes a woman good in bed?" I would say, "A man who is good in bed."

Bob Guccione

I am fed up with men who use sex like a sleeping pill.

Toni Braxton

Honest women are inconsolable for the mistakes they haven't made.

Sacha Guitry

There are no bad women; some are better than others, but there are no bad ones.

Buddy Hackett

If I had my life to live over again, I'd make the same mistakes, only sooner.

Tallulah Bankhead

Keep thy eyes wide open before marriage and half shut afterward.

Thomas Fuller

Quirky is sexy, like scars or chipped teeth. I also like tattoos—they're rebellious.

Jennifer Aniston

Sex is not imaginary, but it is not quite real either.

Mason Cooley

Strong women leave big hickeys.

Madonna

I don't think when I make love.

Brigitte Bardot

Women are meant to be loved, not understood.

Oscar Wilde

My advice to those who think they have to take their clothes off to be a star is once you're boned, what's left to create the illusion? Let 'em wonder.

Mae West

Tits and ass, tits and ass, that's what makes the world go round.
Lenny Bruce

I want a man who's kind and understanding. Is that too much to ask of a millionaire?
Zsa Zsa Gabor

Just saying "no" prevents teenage pregnancy the way "Have a nice day" cures chronic depression.
Faye Wattleton

Chasing the naughty couples down the grassgreen gooseberried double bed of the wood.

Dylan Thomas, *Under Milk Wood*

She [Marilyn Monroe] was our angel...and the sugar of sex came up from her like a resonance of sound in the clearest grain of a violin...a very Stradivarius of sex.

Norman Mailer

What, when drunk, one sees in other women, one sees in Garbo sober.

Kenneth Tynan

Oh what a tangled web we weave when first we practice to conceive. **Don Herold**

A woman is only a woman, but a good cigar is a smoke.

Rudyard Kipling

Sex is a body-contact sport. It is safe to watch but more fun to play.

Thomas Szasz

I am always looking for meaningful one-night stands.

Dudley Moore

There is nothing more interesting in this world to me than my own orgasm…and nothing more boring than yours.

Dennis Miller

Your traditional well-built woman, meaning large breasts, small waist, good butt, good legs. That's my sexual ideal.

John Travolta

There's a broad with her future behind her.

Constance Bennett (of Marilyn Monroe)

I don't think a man is automatically great in bed if he goes on and on for ages. In fact, some of the most exciting times are when you just do it in five minutes.

Cheryl Tiegs

Nobody in their right minds would call me a nymphomaniac. I only sleep with good-looking men.

Fiona Pitt-Kethley

Literature is mostly about having sex and not much about having children; life is the other way round.

David Lodge

Sex is like having dinner: Sometimes you joke about the dishes, sometimes you take the meal seriously.

Woody Allen

Bachelors know more about women than married men. If they did not they would be married, too.

Johann Wolfgang von Goethe

I've always thought it's the role of women to spread sex and sunshine in the lives of men.

Jayne Mansfield

I'm not going to make the same mistake once.

Warren Beatty

It was not the apple on the tree, but the pair on the ground, I believe, that caused the trouble in the garden.

M. D. O'Connor

I wouldn't like to sleep with a guy who was a virgin. I'd have to teach him stuff and I don't have the patience.

Madonna

Nothing in the world makes a woman feel more in command of herself than looking in the mirror and seeing her face surrounded by blond hair.

Lois Wyse

"I'm the kind of girl who's tried everything once," says Valerie Perrine.... But after being with her for a few minutes, you get the idea she's tried a few things twice.

Rex Reed

I want to be liberated and still be able to have a nice ass and shake it.

Shirley MacLaine

It is now quite lawful for a Catholic woman to avoid pregnancy by a resort to mathematics, though she is still forbidden to resort to physics or chemistry.

H. L. Mencken

The legs aren't so beautiful. I just know what to do with them. Marlene Dietrich

Walter Matthau

The first girl you go to bed with is always pretty.

It isn't what I do
but how I do it.
It isn't what I say
but how I say it.
And how I look
when I do it.

Mae West

It's babe power, which means you don't have to look, walk, or act like a man to be his equal.

Diane Brill

The best thing about being in a relationship is having someone right there to do it with when you're horny.

Jenny McCarthy

If all the young girls at the Yale prom were laid end to end, I wouldn't be at all surprised.

Dorothy Parker

I have steak at home. Why go out for hamburger?

Paul Newman

I have the knack of easing scruples.

Molière

Virginity is like a balloon: One prick and it's gone.

Graffito

No one is more carnal than a recent virgin.
John Steinbeck

Experience is the name everybody gives to their mistakes.
Oscar Wilde

People's sex habits are as well-known
in Hollywood as their political opinions,
and much less criticized.
Ben Hecht

I have to find a girl attractive
or it's like trying to start a car
without an ignition key.
Jonathan Aitken

Celibacy is never having
to say you're boring.
Gabrielle Brown

Sex: the poor man's polo.

Clifford Odets

Marriage is a feast where the grace is sometimes better than the dinner.

Charles Caleb Colton

I'll come no more behind your scenes, David [Garrick], for the silk stockings and white bosoms of your actresses excite my amorous passions.

Samuel Johnson

Human beings are infinitely adaptable. If they can do it in the back of a '57 Chevy, they can do it anywhere.

Dr. Patricia Santy (on the possibility of sex in space)

I've tried several varieties of sex. The conventional position makes me claustrophobic and the others give me a stiff neck or lockjaw.

Tallulah Bankhead

I'd like to get married because I like the idea of a man being required by law to sleep with me every night.

Carrie Shaw

The art of love: knowing how to combine the temperament of a vampire with the discretion of an anemone.

E. Michael Cioran

I was wondering what the religion of the country is— and all I could come up with is sex.

Clare Boothe Luce

To go together is blessed; to come together is divine.

Unknown

I like men who have a future and women who have a past.

Oscar Wilde

It's not true that the more sex you have the more it interferes with your work. I find that the more sex you have, the better work you do.

H. G. Wells

The intoxication of rouge is an insidious vintage known to more girls than mere men can ever believe.

Dorothy Speare

Temptation discovers what we are.

Thomas à Kempis

If a woman hasn't a tiny streak of harlot in her, she's as dry as a stick as a rule.

D. H. Lawrence

She's [Debra Winger] naked all through the movie, though she never takes her clothes off.

Pauline Kael

I am too interested in other men's wives to think about getting one of my own.

George Moore

The closest I ever came to a ménage à trois was once when I dated a schizophrenic.

Rita Rudner

Sexual relationships are often like an hourglass: one single point of contact.

Bernard Berenson

He regarded every orgasm as his testimony of love for me.

Britt Ekland (on Rod Stewart)

Sex is the short cut to everything.

Anne Cumming

When you want your boyfriend to play with you, wear a full-length black nightgown with buttons all over it. Sure it's uncomfortable. But it makes you look just like his remote control.

Diana Jordan and Paul Seaburn

I may not be a great actress but I've become the greatest at screen orgasms. Ten seconds of heavy breathing, roll your head from side to side, simulate a slight asthma attack, and die a little.

Candice Bergen

Why should we take advice on sex from the pope? If he knows anything about it, he shouldn't.

George Bernard Shaw

There are a number of mechanical devices which increase sexual arousal, particularly in women. Chief among these is the Mercedes-Benz 380SL.

Lynn Lavner

When grown-ups do it it's kind of dirty.
That's because there is no one
to punish them.

Tuesday Weld

There are only two types of women:
goddesses and doormats.

Pablo Picasso

Home is heaven and orgies are vile,
But you *need* an orgy, once in a while.

Ogden Nash

The only problem with sexually liberating women is that there aren't enough sexually liberated men to go around.

Gloria Steinem

I know there are nights when I have the power, when I put on something and walk in somewhere and if there is a man who doesn't look at me, it's because he's gay.

Kathleen Turner

Three minutes of serious sex and I need eight hours of sleep and a bowl of Wheaties.

Richard Pryor

Sex is like a bank account: After you withdraw you lose interest. Graffito

Give a man a free hand and he'll run it all over you.

Mae West

It isn't premarital sex if you have no intention of getting married.

George Burns

Candy is dandy, but liquor is quicker.

Ogden Nash

Dancing is wonderful training for girls. It's the first way you learn to guess what a man is going to do before he does it.

Christopher Morley

I've made so many movies playing a hooker that they don't pay me in the regular way anymore. They leave it on the dresser.

Shirley MacLaine

Prostitutes for pleasure, concubines for service, wives for breeding.

Sir Richard Burton

Some say that when beauty fades, love goes. Isn't it the other way around? Beauty fades only when love is gone.

Marjorie Holmes

The awful thing about one-night stands is that it is so difficult to keep things tidy.

Anne Cumming

I can't get aroused until I see a pair of rubber dice hanging from the mirror.

Johnny Carson

He and I had an office so tiny that an inch smaller and it would have been adultery.

Dorothy Parker

If it weren't for pickpockets,
I'd have no sex life at all.
Rodney Dangerfield

You see an awful lot of smart guys
with dumb women, but you hardly
ever see a smart woman
with a dumb guy.
Erica Jong

One of the principal differences between a woman and a volcano is that a volcano doesn't fake eruptions.

Tim Dedopulos

I got married, and we had a baby nine months and ten seconds later.

Jayne Mansfield

Scratch most feminists and underneath there is a woman who longs to be a sex object; the difference is that it is not all she longs to be.

Betty Rollins

You have to penetrate a woman's defenses. Getting into her head is a prerequisite to getting into her body.

Bob Guccione

A diamond is the only kind of ice that keeps a girl warm.

Elizabeth Taylor

Girls look forward to college because they wouldn't be obliged to have sex under the football bleachers anymore, but would be able to do it in their own beds.

Ingrid Bengis

Sex, like the city streets, would be risk-free only in totalitarian regimes. Camille Paglia

Unknown

If sex doesn't scare the cat, you're not doing it right.

I'm too shy to express my sexual needs except over the phone to people I don't know.

Garry Shandling

I find lovemaking a serious and delightful occupation.

Winston Churchill

The sex organ has a poetic power, like a comet.

Juan Miró

I haven't heard of girls being attracted by *poor* old men.

Sophia Loren

Women over thirty are at their best, but men over thirty are too old to recognize it.

Jean-Paul Belmondo

The word is legs. . . .Spread the word.

Graffito

Can I cook? Nobody ever asked me to.

Mae West

Uncorseted, her friendly bust
Gives promise of pneumatic bliss.
T. S. Eliot

These days the honeymoon is rehearsed
much more often than the wedding.
P. J. O'Rourke

Condoms aren't completely safe.
A friend of mine was wearing
one and got hit by a bus.
Bob Rubin

His Grace returned from the wars today
and pleasured me twice in his top-boots.
Sarah, 1st Duchess of Marlborough

If you don't have an orgasm daily,
you become very nervous,
very uptight. I do, anyway.
Linda Lovelace

I'm as pure as the driven slush.

Tallulah Bankhead

Wanton kittens make sober cats.

Proverb

We have got to let the mind open *freely*, freely toward sex, and understand from the moment that you're on a date with a man, the idea of sex is *hovering* in the air—*hover, hover, hover*, okay?

Camille Paglia

In lovemaking, feigning lovers succeed much better than the really devoted.

Ninon de Lenclos

In the same way aspirin eases a headache, and penicillin battles the flu, a dose of pornography can work medicinal magic on sufferers of sexual stress.

Dr. Jay Mann

I never expected to see the day when girls would get sunburned in the places they do today.

Will Rogers

I had a very powerful impulse to sexual freedom. One shouldn't be too hard on adultery.

Bertrand Russell

Really that little dealybob is too far away from the hole. It should be built right in.

Loretta Lynn

A bachelor, in my opinion, is only half alive.

Mozart

Men aren't necessities, they're luxuries.

Cher

The borderline between normal and abnormal is by no means sharp, and there are kinds of intermediate stages.

J. Fabricus-Møller

A mistress comes between a mister and his mattress.

Unknown

The natural man has only two primal passions, to get and beget.

William Osler

Now I know what I have been faking all these years.

Private Judy Benjamin (Goldie Hawn)

Do you know many men who would sit still with Marilyn Monroe in their arms?

Simone Signoret

To hear many religious people talk, one would think God created the torso, head, legs, and arms, but the devil slapped on the genitals.

Don Schrader

As far as my attraction to a man is concerned, if his mind works, everything works. That's something I didn't always know.

Sylvie Vartan

If you're contemplating marrying again, Barbara, dear, just remember to rotate your hips. It makes things more pleasant for the man.

Marjorie Hutton

Censorship feeds the dirty mind more than the four-letter word itself.

Dick Cavett

A caress is better than a career.

Elizabeth Marbury

Age does not protect you from love, but love, to some extent, protects you from age.

Jeanne Moreau

Desire is in men a hunger, in women only an appetite.

Mignon McLaughlin

Life in Lubbock, Texas, taught me two things: One is that God loves you and you're going to burn in hell. The other is that sex is the most awful, filthy thing on earth and you should save it for someone you love.

Butch Hancock

Erection is chiefly caused by parsnips, artichokes, turnips, asparagus, candid ginger, acorns bruised to powder and drunk in muscatel, scallion, sea shellfish, etc.
Aristotle

The secret of staying young is to live honestly, eat slowly, sleep sufficiently, work industriously, worship faithfully— and then lie about your age.
Lucille Ball

When you find the place where a woman loves to be fondled, don't you be ashamed to touch it any more than she is.

Ovid

Life without sex might be safer but it would be unbearably dull. It is the sex instinct which makes women seem beautiful, which they are once in a blue moon, and men seem wise and brave, which they never are at all. Throttle it, denaturalize it, take it away, and human existence would be reduced to the prosaic, laborious, boresome, imbecile level of life in an anthill.

H. L. Mencken

Erotica and porn are like sex: Women are more turned on by the foreplay and titillation; men prefer the hard stuff.

Janine di Giovanni

Love's mysteries in souls do grow, But yet the body is his book. John Donne

It is not sex that gives the pleasure, but the lover.

Marge Piercy

Marriage has many pains, but celibacy has no pleasures.

Samuel Johnson

Love is a power too strong to be overcome by anything but flight.

Miguel de Cervantes

I'm like the most expensive, exotic item on a gourmet menu. People can wonder about the sensuous delights of the dish, but they can't afford such an expensive luxury.

Anna Kournikova

For this is one of the miracles of love; it gives—to both, but perhaps especially to the woman—a power of seeing through its own enchantments and yet not being disenchanted.

C. S. Lewis

Many lucky charms are strongly suggestive of the male member. . . . From a historic point of view the mandrake root and the rhinoceros horn have provided the most potent sexual symbols and have thereby gained reputations as powerful aphrodisiacs.

Peter V. Taberner

Let us hope that women never become so liberated that it is impossible to write love poems to them.

Anatole Broyard

The only thing wrong with being an atheist is that there's nobody to talk to during an orgasm.

Unknown

Amo, amass
I loved a lass
And she was tall and slender;
Amas, amat,
I laid her flat
And tickled her feminine gender.
Harry N. Cary

Anything worth doing well
is worth doing slowly.
Gypsy Rose Lee

An Italian will kiss you quickly on the mouth, pressured by his constant search to prove his manhood—elsewhere. A kiss cannot ensure his potency, he will reason, and touch his testicles for the thousandth time that day to make sure they are still there.

Doris Lilly

However carefully you phrase the history of your sex life, you're bound to emerge as a boaster, a braggart, a liar, or a laughingstock.

William Rushton

In the case of some women, orgasms take quite a bit of time. Before signing on with such a partner, make sure you are willing to lay aside, say, the month of June, with sandwiches having to be brought in.

Bruce Jay Friedman

The success of the marriage comes after the failure of the honeymoon.

G. K. Chesterton

The hypothalamus is one of the most important parts of the brain, involved in many kinds of motivation, among other functions. The hypothalamus controls the "Four Fs": fighting, fleeing, feeding, and mating.

Unidentified psychology professor

A woman's chastity consists, like an onion, of a series of coats. Nathaniel Hawthorne

Pierre Auguste Renoir

A painter who has the feel of breasts and buttocks is saved.

In each year with him [Errol Flynn] I packed in more fun, more real living than some wives get in forty years.

Patricia Wymore

An orgy looks particularly alluring seen through the mists of righteous indignation.

Malcolm Muggeridge

Honey, I've never taken up with a congressman in my life.... I've never gone below the Senate.

Barbara Howar

Flirtation is merely an expression of considered desire coupled with an admission of its impracticality.

Marya Mannes

Don't worry,

it only seems kinky the first time.

Unknown

Do infants enjoy infancy as much as adults enjoy adultery?

Murray Banks

It's not how you fish, it's how you wiggle your worm.

Unknown

I found I liked sexual intercourse because of its amazing power of producing a celestial flood of emotion and exaltation of existence.

George Bernard Shaw

In real life, women are always trying to mix something up with sex—religion, or babies, or hard cash; it is only men who long for sex separated out without rings or strings.
Katherine Whitehorn

Tonight after the children are in bed, place a lighted candle on the floor and seduce him under the dining-room table.
Marabel Morgan

Sex means spank and beautiful means bottom.

Kenneth Tynan

Anticipation makes the hard-on longer.

Itsby Stevintary

According to a new survey, women say they feel more comfortable undressing in front of men than they do undressing in front of other women. They say that women are too judgmental, where, of course, men are just grateful.

Robert de Niro

I swear I will be faithful; I could be trusted with fifty virgins naked in a dark room.

Horatio Nelson (to Lady Hamilton)

The buttocks are the most aesthetically pleasing part of the body because they are nonfunctional. Although they conceal an essential orifice, these pointless globes are as near as the human form can ever come to abstract art.

Kenneth Tynan

The beautiful feeling after writing a poem is on the whole better even than after sex, and that's saying a lot.

Anne Sexton

As a young man I used to have four supple members and one stiff one. Now I have four stiff and one supple.

Henri, duc d'Aumale

She [Wallis Simpson, later Duchess of Windsor] could make a matchstick seem like a Havana cigar.

Unknown

The difference between light and hard is that you can sleep with a light on.

Unknown

"Virgin" derives from the Latin *vir* "a man," and *gin* "a trap."

Unknown

Men reach their sexual peak at eighteen. Women reach theirs at thirty-five. Do you get the feeling that God is playing a practical joke?

Rita Rudner

We're all into tight asses and tits that won't hold a pencil under them. Old is like an enemy you have to make peace with before you get there.

Cher

I'm not cheap, but I am on special this week.

Unknown

Take not the first refusal ill:
Tho' now she won't, anon she will.

Thomas D'Urfey

A woman never forgets the men she could
have had; a man, the women he couldn't.

Unknown

All women's dresses are merely variations on the eternal struggle between admitted desire to dress and unadmitted desire to undress.

Lin Yutang

A student undergoing a word-association test was asked why a snowstorm put him in mind of sex. He replied frankly, "Because everything does."

Honor Tracy

Anyone who says that gratuitous sex is no substitute for gratuitous violence obviously hasn't had enough gratuitous sex.

Geoff Spear

When I act I don't make love and when I make love I don't act.

Mae West

There aren't any hard women, just soft men.

Raquel Welch

There is no middle-class sexual style for men. What would it be based on? Golfing? Discussing stock options? Attending church? Downing highballs?

Edmund White

Marital sex develops a routine, but the routines of a stranger are a novelty. Infidelities are a search for novelty, and *dongiovannismo* is more properly a woman's disease than a man's.

Anthony Burgess

I bid all men not to shun but to pursue sweet desire; love is the whetstone of the soul.

Alpheus of Mitylene

A man who is old enough to know better is always on the lookout for a girl who isn't.

Unknown

I once knew a woman who offered her honor
So I honored her offer
And all night long I was on her and off her.
Unknown

Love is not born of
breasts and bottoms alone.
Graham Masterton

Who sleeps with whom is intrinsically more
interesting than who votes for whom.
Malcolm Muggeridge

What women *really* want is three hours of goddamned foreplay.

Dan Greenburg

Despite a lifetime of service to the cause of sexual liberation, I have never caught venereal disease, which makes me feel rather like an Arctic explorer who has never had frostbite.

Germaine Greer

You know very well that love is, above all, the gift of oneself.

Jean Anouilh

Women can always be caught; that's the first rule of the game. Ovid

I don't think pornography is very harmful, but it is terribly, terribly boring.

Noël Coward

All my close friends and relationships have nice asses, come to think of it.

Enrico Vassi

I think sex is better than logic, but I can't prove it.

Unknown

There are two kinds of women: those who want power in the world and those who want power in the bedroom.

Jacqueline Kennedy Onassis

The average man is more interested in a woman who is interested in him than he is in a woman—any woman—with beautiful legs.

Marlene Dietrich

Love is blind, and lovers cannot see
The pretty follies that themselves commit.

William Shakespeare

Like a ski resort full of girls looking for husbands and husbands looking for girls, the situation is not as symmetrical as it might seem.

Alan McKay

Housework is like bad sex. Every time I do it I swear I will never do it again. Until the next time company comes.

Marilyn Sokol

All a man really wants is complete worship and adoration. He knows he's perfect, but he likes to hear it from you.

Zsa Zsa Gabor

For flavor, instant sex will never supersede the stuff you have to peel and cook.

Quentin Crisp

And the world's shrunken to a heap
Of hot flesh straining on a bed.
E. R. Dodds

Orgies are for sexual athletes.
Quentin Crisp

I love sex. It's free and doesn't
require special shoes.
Unknown

Love is like a lion's tooth.
W. B. Yeats

Women are the possessors of the only anatomical part which serves no other function than the simple one of bodily pleasure.

Jeanette Winterton

A liberated woman is one who has sex before marriage and a job after.

Gloria Steinem

Zsa Zsa Gabor got married as a one-off and it was so successful she turned it into a series.

Bob Hope

Of opium, it is well-known that at first it increases sexual activity. Voluptuous fantasies and visions are also characteristic of these stages.

Iwan Bloch

Let's face it, the sex organs ain't got no personality.

Mae West

Like a fierce wind roaring high up in the bare branches of trees, a wave of passion came over me, aimless but surging....I suppose it's lust, but it's awful and holy like thunder and lightning and the wind.

Joanna Field

Sex is something the children never discuss in the presence of their elders. Arthur S. Roche

Jackie Stewart

Cornering is like bringing a woman to a climax.

I only put on clothes so that I'm not naked when I go out shopping.

Julia Roberts

Sex, to paraphrase Clausewitz, is the continuation of war by other means.

Ross Wetzsteon

Sex is like the air: It's not important unless you aren't getting any.

Unknown

Music and women I cannot but give way to, whatever my business is.

Samuel Pepys

Thou shalt not commit adultery ... unless in the mood.

W. C. Fields

If sex isn't a joke, what is?

Nella Larsen

More belongs to marriage than four bare legs in a bed.

Proverb

The game women play is men.
Adam Smith

In a wife I would desire
What in whores is always found—
The lineaments of gratified desire.
William Blake

No one ever died from an
overdose of pornography.
William Margold

During sex I fantasize that I'm someone else.
Richard Lewis

There is nothing safe about sex.
There never will be.
Norman Mailer

It's hard to be funny
when you have to be clean.
Mae West

I read so many bad things about sex that I had to give up reading.

Unknown

Nothing makes you forget about love like sex.

Staci Beasley

If someone has to study a textbook on sexual behavior in order to learn how to make love to his wife or girl, something is wrong with him.

Herbert Marcuse

In order to avoid being called a flirt, she always yielded easily.

Charles Talleyrand

Science is a lot like sex. Sometimes something useful comes of it, but that's not the reason we're doing it.

Richard Feynman

If you don't get it by midnight, chances are you ain't going to get it; and if you do, it ain't worth it.

Casey Stengel

I would rather lie on a sofa than sweep beneath it. No one should waste her time on a treadmill of housework.

Shirley Conran

My husband and I had our best sex during our divorce. It was like cheating on our lawyers.

Priscilla Lopez

Time is short and we must seize those pleasures found above the knees.

Proverb

Sex is identical to comedy in that it involves timing.

Phyllis Diller

Don't be tempted to write a literary masterpiece. Our readers want a sexy story…more plot means less room for sex.

Peter Darvill-Evans

There are only three kinds of women in this world: givers, takers, and destroyers. You really have to watch out for those big destroyers.

Bo Belinsky

A good actress lasts, and sex attraction does not.

Brigitte Bardot

The total deprivation of it produces irritability.
Elizabeth Blackwell

He wondered why sexual shyness, which excites the desire of dissolute women, arouses the contempt of decent ones.
Colette

Platonic relationship: the interval between the introduction and the first kiss.

Sophie Irene Loeb

Sex and golf are the two things you can enjoy even if you're not good at them.

Kevin Costner

Don't bother discussing sex with small children. They rarely have anything to add.

Fran Lebowitz

In love, men are amateurs, women the professionals.

François Truffaut

No woman needs intercourse—few women escape it.

Andrea Dworkin

The perfect lover is one who turns into a pizza at 4:00 a.m.

Charles Pierce

I'm a great lover, I'll bet.

Emo Phillips

The chief occupation of my life has been to cultivate the pleasure of the senses. Nothing has ever meant as much to me as that. Feeling myself born for the fair sex, I have always loved it, and have been loved in return as often as possible.

Casanova

Sexual intercourse began
In nineteen sixty-three
(which was rather late for me)—
Between the end of the Chatterley ban
And the Beatles' first LP.
Philip Larkin

I always thought music was more
important than sex—then I thought if I
don't hear a concert for a year and a
half it doesn't bother me.
Jackie Mason

God will give you
the whole body
orgasm when you
die if you spend
your life in divine
foreplay.

Graffito

If it is your time love will track you down like a cruise missile. If you say "No! I don't want it right now," that's when you'll get it for sure. Love will make a way out of no way. Love is like an exploding cigar which we willingly smoke.

Lynda Barry

A terrible thing happened to me last night again—nothing.

Phyllis Diller

You don't have to hit anybody on the head with four-letter words to be sexy. Eartha Kitt

I rely on my personality for birth control.

Liz Winston

Be good. And if you can't be good, be careful. And if you can't be careful, name it after me.

Unknown

Sex is an urge, love is a desire.

Theodor Reik

More experienced and sensitive lovers enjoy their partner's climactic transports, which they are unable to do if they orgasm simultaneously.

Francis Stubbs

It is an infantile superstition of the human spirit that virginity would be thought a virtue and not the barrier that separates ignorance from knowledge.

Voltaire

The only woman worth seeing undressed is the one you have undressed yourself.

The Duchess of Windsor

There's no holding back. The spotlight is on you. Your partner becomes the musician, playing your body as if it were a precious instrument.

Irene Kassorla

It is a silly question to ask a prostitute why she does it.... These are the highest paid "professional" women in America.

Gail Sheehy

A code of honor: Never approach a friend's girlfriend or wife with mischief as your goal ... unless she's *really* attractive.

Bruce Jay Friedman

What is commonly called love, namely the desire of satisfying a voracious appetite with a certain quantity of delicate white human flesh.

Henry Fielding

may i feel said he
(i'll squeal said she
just once said he)
it's fun said she

(may i touch said he
how much said she
a lot said he)
why not said she

(let's go said he
not too far said she
what's too far said he
where you are said she)

e e cummings

The actor and the streetwalker... the two oldest professions in the world—ruined by amateurs.

Alexander Woollcott

The more women with whom a man has intercourse, the greater will be the benefit he derives from the act.

Ko Hung

There are times not to flirt. When you're sick. When you're with children. When you're on the witness stand.

Joyce Jillson

I bought a condom and put it in my wallet when I was fourteen. By the time I pulled it out to use it, it was older than the girl I was with.

Lewis Grizzard

A sweetheart is a bottle of wine; a wife is a wine bottle.

Baudelaire

The orgasm is the sugar coating with which the Creator (or Nature) has disguised the bitter pill of reproduction.

Paul A. Robinson

The kiss is a wordless articulation of desire whose object lies in the future, and somewhat to the south. Lance Morrow

Graffito

Alimony is the screwing you get for the screwing you got.

Love is just a system for getting someone to call you darling after sex.

Julian Barnes

Every animal is sad after coitus except the human female and the rooster.

Claudius Galen

As the French say, there are three sexes—men, women, and clergymen.

Reverend Sydney Smith

Setting a good example for your children takes all the fun out of middle age.

William Feather

Who ever loved, that loved not at first sight?

Christopher Marlowe

Without nipples, breasts would be pointless.

Jody Nathan

I can remember when the air was clean and sex was dirty.

George Burns

There is not so much difference between the hooker and the non-hooker as one might expect.
Ellis Strong

Never accept rides from strange men, and remember that all men are as strange as hell.
Robin Morgan

Sex is the mathematics urge
sublimated.
M. C. Reed

If a woman is meant to have wrinkles,
they should at least be put on
the soles of her feet.
Ninon de Lenclos

Now he's married, Howard's drillin' for
oil. He's so weak he couldn't hit me with
a paddle if I ran across home plate!
Leo Durocher

A gentleman is a patient wolf.

Henrietta Tiarks

Programming is like sex. One mistake and you have to support it for the rest of your life.

Michael Sinz

It's scary… so personal, giving people the opportunity to see if I'm a good kisser or not. You see, I'm not into sex for the sake of it. I think love scenes are more powerful if it's about communication between two people. It's not about sucking face, it's about emotion.

Patrick Swayze

How idiotic civilization is! Why be given a body if you have to keep it shut up in a case like a rare, rare fiddle.

Katherine Mansfield

A man picks up a tramp because he wants a female companion who is no better than he is. In her company, he doesn't feel inferior. He rewards her by treating her like a lady.

Abigail van Buren

Never be ashamed of passion. If you are strongly sexed, you are richly endowed.

Margaret Sanger

I think naked people are very nice. Posing nude is perhaps the best way of reaching people.

Stella Stevens

Writing is like making love. Don't worry about the orgasm, just concentrate on the process.

Isabel Allende

What comes first in a relationship is lust, then more lust.

Jacqueline Bisset

Sex, unlike war, is far too grave a matter to be left to the privates.

Michael Haaren

Sex is a branch of gastronomy— the best cooks make the best lovers. Every woman soon discovers this.

J. G. Ballard

The first kiss is magic, the second is intimate, the third is routine. After that you just take the girl's clothes off.

Raymond Chandler

sexyquotes

Chastity is
curable, if
detected early.
Unknown

After all, my erstwhile dear,
    My no longer cherished,
Need we say it was not love,
    Just because it perished?
Edna St. Vincent Millay

In Jacqueline's experience, charming out-of-the-way restaurants were frequently attached to out-of-the-way motels.

Elizabeth Peters

A good sex life isn't something you're born with, any more than you're born with the ability to cook, to crochet, or take shorthand.

Graham Masterton

My husband only writes about a certain sort of woman. She looks like Marilyn Monroe and has an IQ of 200.

Miriam Stoppard

Big man, big prick—small man, all prick.

Unknown

Sex is a two-way treat.

Franklin P. Jones

All the cosmetics' names seemed obscenely obvious to me in their promises of sexual bliss. They were all firming or uplifting or invigorating. They made you *tingle*. Or *glow*. Or feel young.

Erica Jong

The Bible contains six admonishments to homosexuals and 362 admonishments to heterosexuals. That doesn't mean that God doesn't love heterosexuals. It's just that they need more supervision.

Lynn Lavner

Why not put up that pane of glass called passion between us? It may distort things at times, but it's wonderfully convenient. But no, we were two of a kind, allies and accomplices. In terms of grammar, I could not become the object, or the subject. He had neither the capacity nor the desire to define our roles in any such way.

Françoise Sagan

Just because there's snow on the roof,
it doesn't mean the boiler has gone out.
Unknown

Beating is decent and can even
be done in church; sex isn't.
Alex Comfort

Fifty percent of the women in this
country are not having orgasms. If that
were true of the male population, it would
be declared a national emergency.
Margo St. James

I have seen the ads for the Wonderbra. Is that really a problem in this country? Men not paying enough attention to women's breasts?

Hugh Grant

Kissing and I mean like, yummy, smacking kissing, is the most delicious, most beautiful, and passionate thing that two people can do, bar none. Better than sex, hands down.

Drew Barrymore

Graze on my lips; and if those hills be dry, stray lower, where the pleasant fountains lie.

Shakespeare

I'm a committed bachelor. One of my favorite oxymorons is *engagement party*.

Scott Roeben

It's pitch, sex is. Once you touch it, it clings to you.

Margery Allingham

Those hot pants of hers were so damned tight, I could hardly breathe.

Benny Hill

Love? I make it constantly but I never talk about it.

Marcel Proust

The main problem with honest women is not how to seduce them, but how to take them to a private place. Their virtue hinges on half-open doors.

Jean Giraudoux

When a man is seen with a lot of women, it's "Oh, which one did he grace?" But if a woman is seen with a lot of men, she's just a slut.

Debra Winger

There is not a man who does not want to be a despot when he's excited.

Marquis de Sade

Madame Bovary is the sexiest book imaginable. The woman's virtually a nymphomaniac but you won't find a vulgar word in the entire thing.

Noël Coward

I will show you a love potion without drug or herb or any witch's spell; if you wish to be loved, love.

Hecato

Sex is the Tabasco sauce which an adolescent national palate sprinkles on every course in the menu.

Mary Day Winn

This is my ultimate fantasy: watching QVC with a credit card while making love and eating at the same time.

Yasmine Bleeth

Sexuality is the bottom line. The way a man is in bed indicates how he feels about the universe.
Suzy Chaffee

However much men say sex is not on their minds all the time, it is—most of the time.
Jackie Collins

My heart cannot be happy even for an hour without love.
Catherine the Great

When the life of the party wants to express the idea of a pretty woman in mime, he undulates his two hands in the air and leers expressively. The notion of a curve is so closely connected to sexual semantics that some people cannot resist sniggering at road signs.

Germaine Greer

Sex is the main factor which attracts anyone to nudity, whatever ostensible reasons may be given out to the world.

George Ryley Scott

Fat men make the best lovers. History is full of examples. Consider Cleopatra's choice of Caesar; he was no lightweight, remember. And it wasn't just hair that attracted Delilah to Samson, it was his remarkable girth.

Peter Ustinov

Don't stay in bed, unless you can make money in bed.

George Burns

My doctor has forbidden me to do the three things I love most in the world—fight bulls, ride horses, and mount women. It's time to go.

Juan Belmonte (final words)

She wore a short skirt and a tight sweater and her figure described a set of parabolas that could cause cardiac arrest in a yak. **Woody Allen**

Barbra Streisand

He's [Ryan O'Neal] great-looking but he's no Einstein.

It's as absurd to say that a man can't love one woman all the time as it is to say that a violinist needs several violins to play the same piece of music.

Honoré de Balzac

Beauty. The power by which a woman charms a lover and terrifies a husband.

Ambrose Bierce

A taste for dirty stories may be said to be inherent in the human animal.

George Moore

Mobile phones are the only subject on which men boast about who's got the smallest.

Neil Kinnock

License my roving hands, and let them go, Before, behind, between, above, below.

John Donne

If somebody makes me laugh, I'm his slave for life.

Bette Midler

> No one has ever written a romance better than we live it.

Lauren Bacall

It wouldn't be a good idea
To let him stay.
When they knew each other better—
Not today.
But she put on her new black knickers
Anyway.

Wendy Cope

Christianity has done a great deal
for love by making a sin of it.
Anatole France

You'll have big green eyes, world-class
breasts, ass that won't quit, and legs
that go all the way up.
Valentine McKee

A young woman who allows herself
to be kissed and caressed goes
the rest of the way as well.
Elizabeth-Charlotte, Duchess of Orléans

Adultery is the application of democracy to love.

H. L. Mencken

Love is the irresistible desire to be irresistibly desired.

Robert Frost

For most people the fantasy is driving around in a big car, having all the chicks you want and being able to pay for it. It has always been, still is, and always will be. Anyone who says it isn't is talking bullshit.

Mick Jagger

A halo has to fall only a few inches to become a noose.

Farmers' Almanac

Saying "no" to someone who has already rummaged through our drawers is tricky—but take heart— even Rome, once sacked, did not have to be sacked again and again.

Quentin Crisp

A woman can be big and still sexy. It depends on how she feels.

Elizabeth Taylor

We Barbie dolls are not supposed to behave the way I do.

Sharon Stone

The only difference between men and boys is the cost of their toys.

Unknown

I only take Viagra when I'm with more than one woman.

Jack Nicholson

Life is a flower of which love is the honey.

Victor Hugo

He who asks is a fool for five minutes, but he who does not remains a fool forever.

Chinese proverb

She had a sulky look to her, and her lips stuck out in a way that made me want to mash them in for her.

James M. Cain

Sex appeal is the keynote of our whole civilization.

Henri Bergson

The sensitive interrelationship between a woman's breasts and the rest of her sex life is not only a bodily thrill, but there is a world of poetic beauty in the longing of a loving woman for the child which melts in mists of tenderness toward her lover.

Marie Stopes

I have always espoused chastity except when one can no longer resist the temptation.

Edna O'Brien

The fact is that there hasn't been a thrilling new erogenous zone discovered since de Sade.

George Gilder

If you want to improve sex, ask, "What do you enjoy? What do you feel? Because I care."

William Masters

On a sofa upholstered in panther skin
Mona did research in original sin.

William Plomer

The brain is viewed as an appendage of the genital glands.

Carl Jung

Statistics are like a bikini. What they reveal is suggestive but what they conceal is vital.

Aaron Levenstein

My brain is my second favorite organ.

Woody Allen

I can never understand why most people have sex so quickly. You'd think they didn't enjoy it, the way they plunge in, thrash up and down, and then turn their backs on each other and go to sleep.

Graham Masterton

Over that love affair, scrappy and clamorous,
Time throws a veil iridescent and glamorous,
Cloaking the sordid, revealing the amorous—
Hiding the ashes but leaving the flame.
Edwin Meade Robinson

Jim Morrison is so handsome.
I heard some girl say he was so
good-looking even his face slept around.
Craig Kee Strete

At the touch of love everyone becomes a poet.
Plato

I don't like females all dressed up. Eve in her original state is my ideal: natural, undecorated, modest without Puritanism.

Sean Connery

Infatuation is when you think that he's as sexy as Robert Redford, as smart as Henry Kissinger, as noble as Ralph Nader, as funny as Woody Allen, and as athletic as Jimmy Connors. Love is when you realize that he's as sexy as Woody Allen, as smart as Jimmy Connors, as funny as Ralph Nader, as athletic as Henry Kissinger, and nothing like Robert Redford—but you'll take him anyway.

Judith Viorst

The art of life lies in taking pleasures as they pass, and the keenest pleasures are not intellectual, nor are they always moral.

Aristippus

Some mornings, it's just not worth chewing through the leather straps. **Emo Phillips**

He looks like he's got a cheese danish stuffed in his pants!

Tom Wolfe

Love is a dream, wholly subjective. People fall in love with the most extraordinary people.

Nancy Mitford

Porfirio Rubirosa, the literally priapic rogue and liar whose member was said to be so large that waiters in Paris referred to large pepper mills as Rubirosas.

New York Observer

She was a lovely girl. Our courtship was fast and furious—I was fast and she was furious.

Max Kauffman

Censorship reflects society's lack of confidence in itself.

Potter Stewart

The true feeling of sex is that of a deep intimacy, but above all of a deep complicity.

James Dickey

If venereal delight and the power of propagating the species were permitted only to the virtuous, it would make the world very good.

James Boswell

Sacks? The greatest thing in the world. Oh, sacks? I thought you said sex. Sacks are the second-best thing.

Tom Keating

In reality, despite the daydreams of many men, females rarely force sexual intercourse on males.

C. H. McCaghy

A man must be potent and orgasmic to ensure the future of the race. A woman only needs to be available.

Masters and Johnson

Generally speaking, it is in love
as it is in war, where the longest
weapon carries it.
John Leland

A lover teaches a wife all that her
husband has concealed from her.
Honoré de Balzac

The love bird is 100 percent faithful to
his mate, as long as they are locked
together in the same cage.
Will Cuppy

Sex has become one of the most discussed subjects of modern times. The Victorians pretended it did not exist; the moderns pretend that nothing else exists.

Archbishop Fulton J. Sheen

For it is a maxim I have learned to trust with all my heart that everyone without exception enjoys a sexual life far more active and more rewarding than can be guessed at even by his close friends.

Brendan Gill

We all know girls do it. But if you ask them to do it, they say no. Why? Because they want to be proper. Finally, after thirteen years of courtship and dates and so on, one night they get drunk and they do it. And *after* they've done it, that's all they want to do. Now they're fallen, now they're disgraced, and all they want is to do it. You say, "Let's have a cup of tea." "No, let's do it." "Let's go to the cinema." "No, I'd rather do it."

Mel Brooks

The average male thinks about sex every eleven minutes while he's awake.

Dr. Patrick Greene

It is difficult enough making friends with your own sex, let alone deciding to spend your life with someone of the opposite sex. It is not easy to be interested—and marriage means to be interested—in someone else all the time.

Katharine Hepburn

Seduction is always more singular and sublime than sex, and it commands the higher price.
Jean Baudrillard

Phyllis Diller

His finest hour lasted a minute and a half.

Playboy is sex, closely linked to great business success—and those are the two great Puritan hang-ups.

Hugh Hefner

Is there any greater or keener pleasure than physical love? No, nor any which is more unreasonable.

Plato

Marriage may often be a stormy lake, but celibacy is almost always a muddy horse-pond.

Thomas Love Peacock

You know, of course, that the Tasmanians, who never committed adultery, are now extinct.

W. Somerset Maugham

Sex hasn't been the same since women started enjoying it.

Lewis Grizzard

Here's to wives and sweethearts . . . may they never meet.

John Bunny

The real theater of the sex war is the domestic hearth.

Germaine Greer

In the sex war thoughtlessness is the weapon of the male, vindictiveness of the female.
Cyril Connolly

While we have sex in the mind, we truly have none in the body.
D. H. Lawrence

Which one of us is not suspended by a thread above carnal anarchy, and what is that thread but the light of day?
John Cheever

I don't mind living in a man's world as long as I can be a woman in it.
Marilyn Monroe

Quite a few women told me, one way or another, that they thought it was sex, not youth, that's wasted on the young.
Janet Harris

I have always detested the belief that sex is the chief bond between man and woman. Friendship is far more human.

Agnes Smedley

There's no substitute for moonlight and kissing.

Barbara Cartland

When I first saw the [Niagara] falls I was disappointed in the outline. Every American bride is taken there, and the sight must be one of the earliest, if not the keenest, disappointments of American married life.

Oscar Wilde

Give me some music—music, moody food of us that trade in love…

Cleopatra (from *Antony and Cleopatra*)

I wouldn't give up one minute of my time with Richard Burton. . . . We were like magnets, alternating pulling toward each other and inexorably pushing away.

Elizabeth Taylor

I was a good young man and I'm glad to say it's enabled me to be a wicked old one.

W. Somerset Maugham

Much of man's sex is in his mind, while woman's is more centrally located.

Page Smith

When an old man marries a young wife, he grows younger—but she gets older.

Proverb

Leaving sex to the feminists is like letting your dog vacation at the taxidermist.

Camille Paglia

A wise woman never yields by appointment.

Stendhal

The human spirit sublimates the impulses it thwarts; a healthy sex life mitigates the lust for other sports.

Piet Hein

I'm into cotton underwear. I don't need cheetah-print leather to make me feel sexy.

Nelly Furtado

The greatest provocations of lust are from the apparel.

Robert Burton

Fastidiousness is the ability to resist a temptation in the hope that a better one will come along later.
Oscar Wilde

How love the limb-loosener sweeps me away.
Sappho

Pornography is more than nudey magazines; it is a prevailing atmosphere of sexual license.

Jerry Falwell

To read newspapers and magazines, you would think we were almost worshipping the female bosom.

Billy Graham

Men play the game; women know the score.

Roger Woddis

Love, and do what you like.

St. Augustine

The most popular image of the female despite the exigencies of the clothing trade is all boobs and buttocks, a hallucinating sequence of parabolas and bulges.

Germaine Greer

What is peculiar to modern societies is not that they consigned sex to a shadow existence, but that they dedicated themselves to speaking of it ad infinitum, while exploiting it as the secret.

Michel Foucault

Facing our sexual fantasies honestly would tell us a lot about ourselves.

André Guindon

However muted its present appearance may be, sexual domination obtains nevertheless as perhaps the most pervasive ideology of our culture and provides its most fundamental concept of power.

Kate Millett

A man is as good as he has to be,
and a woman as bad as she dares.
Elbert Hubbard

Up with petticoats, down with drawers!
You tickle mine and I'll tickle yours!
Folk rhyme

Of all the forms of caution,
caution in love is perhaps
most fatal to true happiness.
Bertrand Russell

I lose my respect for the man who can make the mystery of sex the subject of a coarse jest, yet when you speak earnestly and seriously on the subject, is silent.

Henry David Thoreau

I know many married men, I even know a few happily married men, but I don't know one who wouldn't fall down the first open coal-hole running after the first pretty girl who gave him a wink.

George Jean Nathan

Nothing is either all masculine or all feminine except having sex.

Marlo Thomas

Men always fall for frigid women because they put on the best show. Fanny Brice

Men seldom make passes at a girl who surpasses.

Franklin P. Jones

It takes a lot of experience for a girl to kiss like a beginner.

Ladies' Home Journal, 1948

Sex is a discovery.

Fannie Hurst

Each coming together of man and wife, even if they have been mated for many years, should be a fresh adventure; each winning should necessitate a fresh wooing.

Marie Stopes

The omnipresent process of sex, as it is woven into the whole texture of our man's or woman's body, is the pattern of all the process of our life.

Havelock Ellis

You're never too old to become younger.

Mae West

We didn't think of it as a sex scene. We approached it as two characters really getting what they needed. They needed that like they needed air to breathe.

Halle Berry

I think you're running into a lot of trouble if your idea of foreplay is, "Brace yourself honey, here I come!"

Dr. Phil McGraw

Were it not for imagination, sir, a man would be as happy in the arms of a chambermaid as of a duchess.

Samuel Johnson

We might as well make up our minds that chastity is no more a virtue than malnutrition.

Alex Comfort

A maid that laughs is half taken.
Proverb

The genitals themselves have not undergone the development of the rest of the human form in the direction of beauty.
Sigmund Freud

I'm married, but I don't wear a wedding ring because I've found that it tends to give women the impression that I'm unavailable.
Bill Muse

Ever since my childhood I have been accustomed to see the face of every man who has passed me light up with desire. Many women will be disgusted to hear that I have always taken this as homage. Is it despicable to be the flower whose perfume people long to inhale, the fruit they long to taste?

Caroline (la Belle) Otero

If you wish women to love you, be original; I know a man who used to wear felt boots summer and winter, and women fell in love with him.

Anton Chekhov

The problem is that for women, the average time is just over fourteen minutes.... Men are left with about twelve minutes during which time they need to think of something to do!

Dr. Phil McGraw

He's [Marlon Brando]
more than a man.
He's an experience.

Bianca Jagger

Full nakedness, all joys are due to thee,
As souls unbodied, bodies unclothed must be,
To taste whole joys.

John Donne

Men lose more conquests by their own
awkwardness than by any virtue in the woman.
Ninon de Lenclos

Mae West

When women go wrong, men go right after them.

You can judge a politician by the extent to which you can imagine him (or her) having an orgasm. Thus the popularity of John F. Kennedy.

Timothy Leary

He must have had a magnificent build before his stomach went in for a career of its own.

Margaret Halsey

A man does not look behind the door unless he has stood there himself.

Henri du Bois

An erection is a mysterious thing. There's always that fear, each time one goes, that you won't be seeing it again.

Kirk Douglas

An orgasm is just a reflex, like a sneeze.

Ruth Westheimer

If he [Cary Grant] can talk, I'll take him.

Mae West

Never let a kiss
fool you and never
let a fool kiss you.

Betty Grable

Some men say their erections aren't
as big as they recall them once being.
But then their partner says, "Well, dear,
you overestimated them back then, too."

Dr. Paul T. Costa

He kissed the plump mellow yellow smellor melons of her rump, on each plump molonous hemisphere, in their mellow yellow furrow, with obscure prolonged provocation melons mellonous osculation.

James Joyce

Pornography is indefinable, and as irrepressible as prostitution.

Charles Skilton

Perhaps it was time to stretch a bit. The truth is, I didn't want to do those glamorous leading man roles forever. I'm much better at playing villains, or slightly villainous guys. It's more fun and it's definitely more sexy.

Michael Douglas

Women are most fascinating between the ages of thirty-five and forty after they won a few races and know how to pace themselves. Since few ever pass forty, maximum fascination can continue indefinitely.

Christian Dior

If we have to kiss Hollywood goodbye, it may be with one of those tender, old-fashioned, seven-second kisses as exchanged between two people of the opposite sex with all their clothes on.

Anita Loos

If I had my choice, I would marry Roger Moore but have Sean Connery as my lover. He has a cross between menace and humor in his eyes. And a very chewable bottom lip.

Lois Maxwell

A man's heart may have a secret sanctuary where only one woman may enter, but it is full of little anterooms which are still vacant.

Helen Rowland

Modern man isn't as virile as he used to be. Instead of making things happen, he waits for things to happen to him. He goes with the current. Something . . . has led him to stop swimming upstream.

Marcello Mastroianni

All really great lovers are articulate, and verbal seduction is the surest road to actual seduction.

Marya Mannes

It was not a bosom to repose upon, but it was a capital bosom to hang jewels upon.

Charles Dickens

The man's desire is for the woman. The woman's desire is for the desire of the man.

Samuel Taylor Coleridge